D1391591

First published in the UK in 2005 by
Chrysalis Children's Books
An imprint of Chrysalis Books Group Plc
The Chrysalis Building, Bramley Road, London W10 6SP

ISBN 1 84458 185 3

British Library Cataloguing in Publication Data
for this book is available from the British Library.

Senior editor *Rasha Elsaeed*
Project editor *Debbie Foy*
Editorial assistant *Camilla Lloyd*
Food consultant *Brenda Alden*
Art director *Sarah Goodwin*
Illustrator *Molly Sage*
Designer *Ben Ruocco, Tall Tree Ltd*
Picture researchers *Sarah Stewart-Richardson, Veneta Bullen, Miguel Lamas*

Printed in China

10 9 8 7 6 5 4 3 2 1

Words in **bold** can be found in Words to remember on page 30.

Typography *Natascha Frensch*
Read Regular, Read Smallcaps and Read Space; European Community Design Registration 2003
and Copyright © Natascha Frensch 2001-2004 Read Medium, **Read Black** and *Read Slanted*
Copyright © Natascha Frensch 2003-2004

READ™ is a revolutionary new typeface that will enhance children's understanding through clear, easily
recognisable character shapes. With its evenly spaced and carefully designed characters, READ™ will help
children at all stages to improve their literacy skills, and is ideal for young readers, reluctant readers and
especially children with dyslexia.

Picture Acknowledgements
All reasonable efforts have been made to ensure the reproduction of content has been done with the consent
of copyright owners. If you are aware of any unintentional omissions please contact the publishers directly so
that any necessary corrections may be made for future editions.

Anthony Blake Photo Library: Joy Skipper FC, 21B, Georgia Glynn Smith; akg-images: Erich Lessing 6; Alamy
Images: Ian Dagnall 18B, Foodfolio 20; British Free Range Egg Producers Association: 11, 12, 15, 18T; Chrysalis
Image Library: 21T, Ray Moller 24T, 24B, 25; Corbis: Wolfgang Kaehler 9T, Tom Stewart 26, Roy Morsch 27;
Frank Lane Picture Agency: F.Lanting/Minden Pictures 9B, Hans Dieter Brandl 10, Silvestris Fotoservice 13;
Getty Images: Miki Duisterhof 8; Holt Studios: Nigel Cattlin 1, 16, 17, Rosie Mayer 19; Rex Features: Organic
Picture Library 4, Sunset 23; Scala Archives: ©Photo SCALA, Florence/British Museum 7; Scottish Egg
Producer Retailers Association: BC, 14.

Contents

What is an egg?

Animals such as ducks, reptiles, insects and some fish lay eggs when they give birth to young.

These eggs have recently been laid by hens.

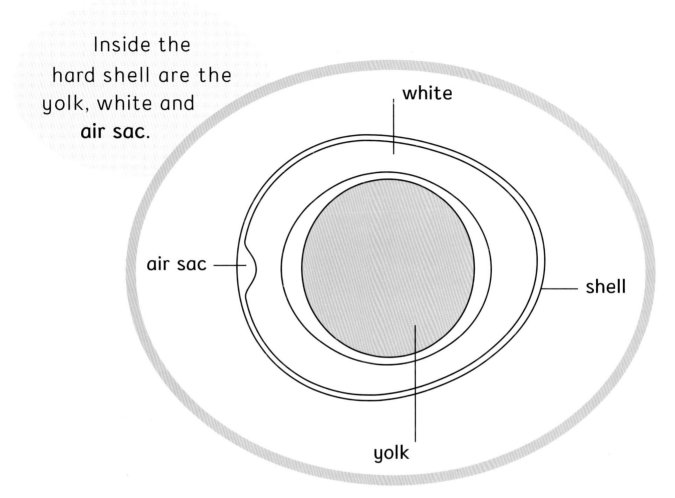

Inside the hard shell are the yolk, white and **air sac**.

white

air sac

shell

yolk

An egg contains everything a **newborn** animal needs to grow. If a hen's egg is **fertilised**, a chick will grow inside. If it is not fertilised, then we can eat the egg.

Back in time

Eggs are one of the earliest known food sources. People began to eat eggs that they found on the ground, probably **abandoned** from birds' nests.

These paintings tell us that the ancient Egyptians hunted birds for their eggs.

They learnt that hens' eggs could be eaten and so they **domesticated** hens. This meant they could have eggs to eat every day.

This Greek **sculpture** shows the goddess Hera holding a chicken and egg.

All sorts of eggs

The most common eggs we eat are from hens, but we can eat duck, **quail** and **ostrich** eggs, too.

Eggs can be brown, white, green or blue depending on the **breed** of hen.

Quails' eggs are smaller than hens' eggs and are green or blue with **speckles**.

Eggs that you find in birds' nests should not be eaten as they contain chicks.

Ostrich eggs are large as they are the biggest birds in the world.

Hens

Hens start to lay eggs when they are about five months old. They can lay for up to five years, but they have long gaps between **broods**.

Fertilised eggs will develop into chicks.

Hens will often lay an egg a day or up to 300 eggs each year. They are fed wheat and **soya** with added **vitamins**.

As a rule, brown hens lay brown eggs and white hens lay white eggs.

Hens are fed by the farmer and given water throughout the day.

Laying eggs

The eggs we eat are from hens that are caged, live in barns or are **free range**. Caged hens are kept on a **factory farm**.

These hens live on an **organic** farm where they are free to **roam** around.

Barn hens are also kept in cages but they are able to move around for part of the day. Free-range hens live in barns and can roam outdoors.

Factory-farmed hens live in cages with sloping floors. Their eggs roll into a tray for collection.

To see if an egg is good to eat, lower it into a bowl of salted water. A fresh egg will sink but a bad egg will float.

Collecting eggs

When the eggs have been laid they are collected. In some farms, they roll onto a **conveyor belt** into the sorting room. In other farms, they are collected by hand.

This free-range farmer is collecting eggs by hand.

Every two to three days the eggs are taken to the packing centre.

Eggs should always be stored in a fridge with their pointed ends downwards.

Each egg is checked to ensure it is not broken.

Grading and packing

At the packing centre, the eggs are **graded** and packed. The eggs are checked again to make sure they are good enough for people to eat.

Eggs are packed into cardboard trays and boxes to protect them.

Each egg is weighed and packed into a carton according to its size. We can buy small, medium, large or very large eggs.

Rare double-yolk eggs come from young hens that are not used to laying.

Egg boxes show the size, **sell-by date** and kind of eggs.

Getting to you

Egg boxes are wrapped to protect the eggs and loaded onto a lorry. Eggs break easily so they must be handled carefully.

Lorries take the eggs from the factory to shops and **wholesalers**.

This local market stall in Spain sells a variety of fresh eggs.

When an egg is laid, it can take just two to three days for it to reach your table!

Some people keep their own hens so they can have fresh eggs every day.

Eating eggs

There are many ways to cook and eat eggs. They can be **hard-boiled** or **soft-boiled**, **poached**, scrambled or fried.

Soft-boiled eggs are good eaten with **toasted soldiers**.

Eggs will last up to a month kept in the fridge. You can use eggs to make omelettes, custards, flans, soufflés and mayonnaise or simply eat them on their own.

To scramble eggs, stir them with milk and melted butter over a low heat until they set.

To poach eggs, break them into a small pan of **simmering** water.

Everyone loves eggs

People around the world enjoy eggs and many countries have their own special egg recipes. In Spain they make tortilla using eggs, potatoes and vegetables.

A frittata is made with eggs, cheese, tomatoes and herbs.

Meringues are made by beating egg whites then cooking them. Australians cover meringues in fresh cream and strawberries to make a pavlova.

Eggs that are not turned over during frying are called 'sunny side up'.

In Italy they sometimes break eggs onto pizzas.

23

A balanced diet

Eggs are a good source of **protein** and are extremely nutritious. They also contain vitamins and **minerals**, such as calcium.

Other foods rich in protein are meat, fish, beans and nuts.

Fruit and vegetables contain **carbohydrates** and provide lots of vitamins and **fibre**.

For a balanced diet, most of the food we eat should come from the groups at the bottom of the chart and less from the top.

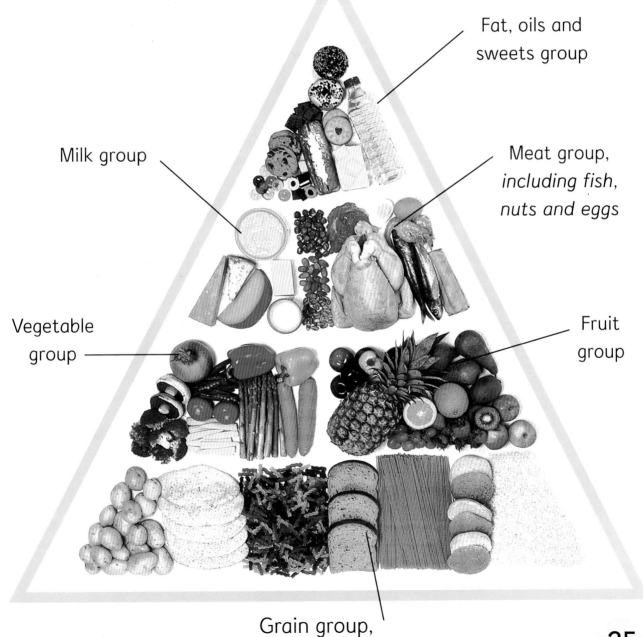

Fat, oils and sweets group

Milk group

Meat group, *including fish, nuts and eggs*

Vegetable group

Fruit group

Grain group, *including potatoes*

Healthy eggs

The protein in eggs is essential for growth and repair. It is also important for our body's development.

When we fall and cut ourselves, protein helps to heal the wound.

The vitamins and calcium in eggs are needed for healthy bones, teeth, skin and hair.

Protein and calcium are needed to keep growing children healthy.

Egg wheelies

Make lunchtime fun with these delicious egg wheelies. They are easy to make and really good for you! Serves 2

Children in the kitchen must be supervised at all times by an adult.

YOU WILL NEED

- 2 large eggs, hard-boiled
- 3 slices wholemeal bread, crusts removed
- Soft butter or margarine
- 15g/1 tablespoon mayonnaise and 15g/1 tablespoon plain, low-fat yoghurt, mixed together
- Cress

1. Remove the shells from the eggs and chop them finely.

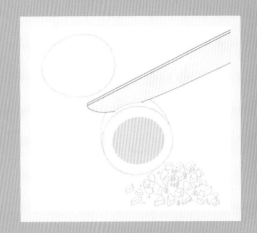

2. Mash the eggs and the mayonnaise and yoghurt mixture together in a bowl.

3. Spread butter on one side of the bread slices, then spread a thin layer of egg mixture on a slice of bread. Add some cress.

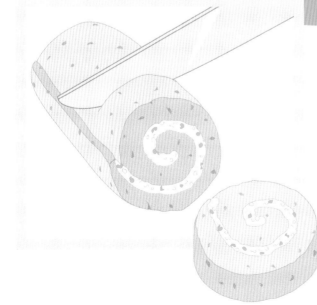

4. Roll the bread tightly then slice it lengthwise in to four 'wheels'. Repeat for each slice of bread.

Words to remember

air sac A pocket of air that is formed in the egg after laying.

abandoned Something that is left behind and not taken care of anymore.

breed A type of animal within an animal group.

brood A group of young animals born to the same mother at the same time.

carbohydrate Nutrient the body needs for energy.

conveyor belt A machine that carries things along.

domesticated When an animal is brought up among humans.

factory farm Where animals are bred and kept for food.

fertilised A fertilised egg will produce young that grow into adults.

fibre Material found in plants and grains that helps digestion.

free range When farm animals are allowed to roam freely.

graded The quality of something.

hard-boiled An egg boiled in water until the yolk is firm.

minerals Nutrients the body needs for good health and to prevent illness.

newborn When an animal emerges from its mother or egg into the world.

organic Plants or animals that live without the use of chemicals.

ostrich The largest bird in the world.

poached To cook gently in simmering water.

protein A nutrient needed for growth and repair.

quail A small, round bird with a short tail.

roam To walk freely around.

sculpture Carved figures in stone, wood or metal.

sell-by-date The date by which food must be sold from the shop.

simmering To slowly cook on a medium-to-low heat.

soft-boiled To boil an egg for a short time so that the yolk is still runny.

soya A type of protein.

speckles Small spots or patches of colour.

toasted soldiers Toast that has been buttered and cut into lengths.

vitamins Nutrients we need for good health and to prevent illness.

wholesalers Where shopkeepers go to buy a range of foods to sell.

Index